ACTION SCIENCE

PONDS AND STREAMS

Judith Court

Series Consultant: Joyce Pope

80681

Franklin Watts

London   New York   Toronto   Sydney

© 1985 Franklin Watts Ltd

First published in Great
Britain in 1985
by Franklin Watts Ltd
12a Golden Square
London W1

First published in the United
States of America by
Franklin Watts Inc.
387 Park Avenue South
New York
N.Y. 10016

Phototypeset by Tradespools
Ltd, Frome, Somerset
Printed in Italy

UK edition:
ISBN O 86313 220 0
US edition:
ISBN 0-531-04952-3
Library of Congress
Catalog Card Number:
84-52006

Designed by
Ben White

Illustrated by
Colin Newman, Val Sangster/
Linden Artists,
and Chris Forsey

J
551.48
COU

C 1. Ponds

2. Streams

ACTION
SCIENCE

PONDS AND STREAMS

Contents

Equipment

As well as a few everyday items you will need the following equipment to carry out the activities in this book.

Washing-up bowl	Ruler
Ice-cream container	Tape measure
Margarine containers	Pencils
Jam jars	Notebook
Sieve	Hand lens
Wooden pole	Ball of string
Strong wire	Cotton thread
Net curtain material	Indicator paper
Scotch tape	Eye dropper
Old soup can	Polaroid sunglasses
Plastic spoon	Level

Introduction

Ponds and streams teem with life and you can easily find many different kinds of animal if you know how and where to look. Some creatures look very frightening at first but you will soon learn which ones are harmless and which might give you a bite if you frighten them.

As rainwater drains downhill it carves a channel in the land and so a stream is formed. Ponds appear wherever water is trapped and unable to drain away. Many ponds have been created as a source of water for farm animals. There are a great variety of ponds and streams. Look for changes made where streams have been cleared for better drainage. Recently many ponds have been filled in but your interest could prevent this happening. Perhaps on the other hand you might even be lucky enough to become involved in making a new pond.

Ponds and streams can be dangerous places so it is best to share your investigations with a friend. It is not always easy to guess the depth of water or how firm the bottom is, so always test with a pole before you wade in. Always wear rubber boots or old sneakers. Do not risk bare feet as it is easy to cut your feet on sharp stones or pieces of glass. Remember that most pond and stream water is not clean. Always wash your hands after an investigation.

Investigating a pond

The best time to start a pond study is in early spring before the plants begin to grow. Most animals are not very active at this time and birds have not yet started to build their nests, so you will not disturb them.

You will need to get to know the area by walking around the pond. Try to keep to the same path to avoid trampling too many plants. You can then choose likely places for observing animals. If you use binoculars always remember to have the sun behind you.

When you feel you really know the area well you can draw a plan on graph paper to show the shape of the pond. Put major landmarks like trees or islands on it and show the type of banks that your pond has.

▽ On your visits to the pond record any animals you see in your notebook, together with the time of day and the date. This diary will tell you when animals are most active and how the area changes with the seasons.

6

▽ For a clearer view of underwater life you can make a pond viewer as shown below. Put the covered end into the water and look through the open one.

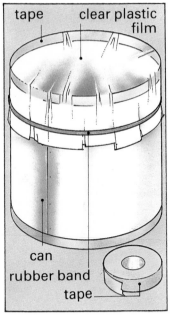

tape   clear plastic film

can
rubber band
tape

△ To make a pond viewer take a large can and use a can opener to remove the top and bottom. Tape the cut edges and use a rubber band to hold a piece of clear plastic over one end.

Pond safari

When you've drawn a plan to show the land around the pond you can take a closer look at the water. Watch the surface for movement. Many creatures are able to use the surface film to support their bodies. Look for water striders skimming along and tiny springtails bouncing on the surface. Whirligig beetles spin around like dodgems on the water as they search for food. All these creatures dart away the moment the surface of the water is disturbed.

When you have looked at surface animals, try to find out what is happening in the water. A pond viewer is very useful for watching free-swimming pond creatures like water boatmen, backswimmers and red water mites. Daphnia and Cyclops swim rapidly in bursts to "jump" through the water, which is why they are often called "water fleas." Using a viewer is like looking through a window into the pond and being on a pond safari.

7

Pond creatures

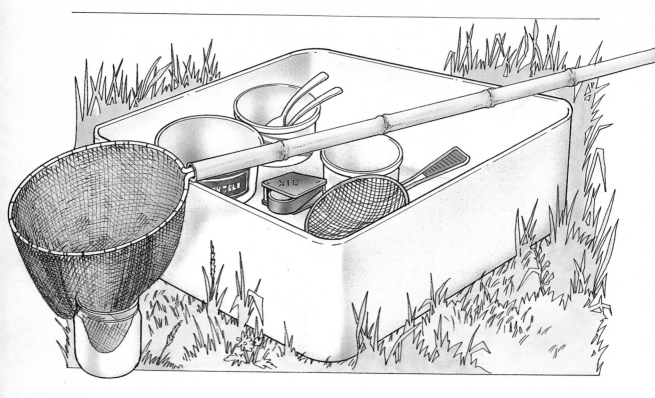

As well as your pond kit you will need a net. You could buy a net or ask an adult to help you make one from a piece of old net curtain material, sewn on to a loop of strong wire. Bind the wire tightly with string to a piece of wooden dowel or a short broom handle. Use a fine flour sieve if you have no net material.

Sweep the net or sieve through the water and empty the contents into the large container of water. Sort out your "catch" by transferring the animals to the smaller containers using a plastic teaspoon.

Pond creatures like to hide, so don't put any weeds, dead leaves, sticks or stones into the containers. Now the animals are easier to view, take closer look using a hand lens. A field guide will help you to identify them.

△ To make a pond kit collect together small white plastic containers, jam jars, a plastic teaspoon, a flour sieve or tea-strainer and a hand lens. Fit these into a large ice-cream container which can be used when you first dip. The white surfaces of your containers help you to see the animals clearly.

8

Skimmers and swimmers

Different animals keep to particular areas of the pond. If you dip with your net half in the water, you will collect those animals which live on or hang just below the surface. These are known as skimmers and air-breathing swimmers.

Diving beetles and backswimmers come regularly to the surface to replenish the bubble of air they carry on their bodies. They do this because they cannot get enough oxygen to breathe from the water, although their larvae have gills and live entirely in the water.

Some other insects, like dragonflies, damselflies and mayflies also lay their eggs in the water. On hatching these become nymphs which have gills to absorb oxygen dissolved in the water. Look at the variety of swimming styles used by nymphs.

▽ You can now take a closer look at the animals supported by the water surface film and those which hang below it. The larvae of gnats and mosquitoes which have hatched from floating rafts of eggs hang from the surface.

Backswimmers, water boatmen and diving beetles swim through the water as do nymphs of dragonflies and mayflies.

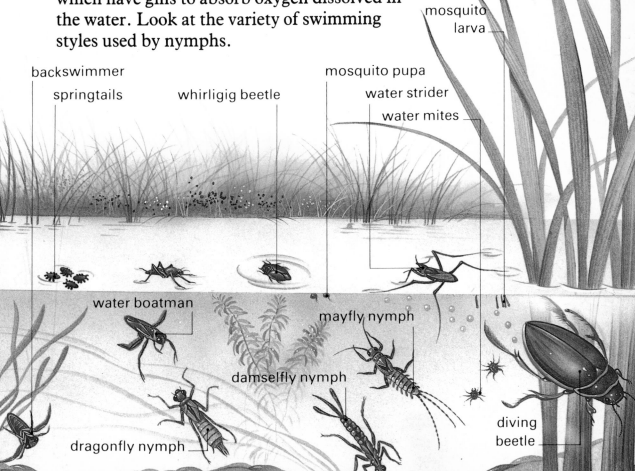

damselfly

mosquito larva

backswimmer

springtails

whirligig beetle

mosquito pupa

water strider

water mites

water boatman

mayfly nymph

damselfly nymph

dragonfly nymph

diving beetle

Dip your net among the weeds and you'll find the animals that cling to their leaves. You will see different kinds of snails. The freshwater winkle has a "door" to close the entrance to its shell. Most snails have shells with pointed spires but the wheel snail has flat whorls.

Snails are herbivores and feed on the green surface film of algae that coats most submerged objects. You can watch grazing snails through the clear glass of a jam jar. The snail moves over the water plants using its strong muscular foot.

Many insects lay their eggs in pondweed. These hatch into larvae or nymphs that hide and hunt among the plants. Dragonfly nymphs are predators that feed on small animals by using jaws attached to a hinged arm. They are the real dragons of the pond who attack insects, tadpoles and small fish.

▽ When leaves and twigs fall into a pond they drop to the bottom and start to rot. Many tiny organisms like bacteria and fungi break down the plant material and provide a source of food for many creatures which stay on the bottom of the pond.

Only those animals that need little oxygen live down here. Some, like bloodworms, can store oxygen in their bodies.

orb snail

water louse

caddisfly larva

leech

flatworms

bloodworms

water mites

▷ Collect fresh-water clams and put them in a dish containing sand and water. They have two hinged shells which open to allow the "foot" and siphons to emerge.

You will be able to watch how they move and see the tracks they make in the sand. Snails make similar trails in mud at the bottom of a bowl of water.

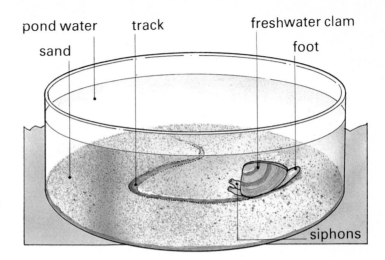

pond water   track   freshwater clam
sand   foot
siphons

Crawlers and clingers

Water lice crawl over the surface of the dead leaves and stones at the bottom of the pond. Together with the flatworms they feed on decaying remains.

Caddisfly larvae are scavengers. They build cases from sand, shells or bits of pondweed. Some animals, like leeches, cling to the surface of stones using suckers at the head and tail end. They move by looping along. They are carnivores feeding on other animals, especially snails.

Keep your bottom dip until last as it stirs up the mud and makes it difficult to see any animals. Use the sieve to hold the catch while washing off the mud.

You might find freshwater clams which are able to cope with muddy conditions. They feed by sucking in water through a tube called a siphon and straining out bits for food. The cleared water is pumped out through a second tube.

When you have finished looking at the animals always return them to the pond by floating them on to a spoon. Do not pick them up in your fingers.

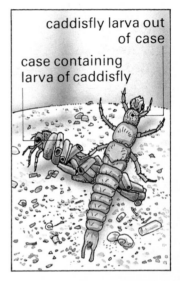

caddisfly larva out of case

case containing larva of caddisfly

△ Persuade a caddisfly larva to come out of its case by gently pushing a piece of grass stem into the case at the tail end.

Place the larva in a dish of pond water containing bits which are like those that made its original case. It will make a new case. The caddisfly larvae use lots of different materials like fine sand, tiny shells and bits of root to make new cases.

11

Pond plants

▷ Different plants grow in bands around the pond depending on the dampness of the ground. Plants in the outer band like marshy conditions. The middle band consists of those with their roots in water. In the center are plants that only grow in or on open water.

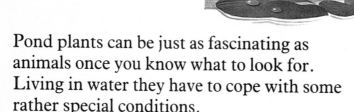

Pond plants can be just as fascinating as animals once you know what to look for. Living in water they have to cope with some rather special conditions.

The commonest pond plants are rushes and sedges. Clumps of these plants are always found in damp places. Rushes have round, spiky stems filled with white fluffy pith. They are smooth, with no leaves and bear bunches of brown flowers.

Sedges have similar flower spikes and tough pointed leaves which grow out in three directions from a triangular stem. These plants form a dense band along the edge of the pond. Among them you may see the violet blue flag.

Aquatic plants

Plants which live in the open water can be divided into three groups. On the surface of the water you will find plants like duckweed known as free-floaters or floating aquatics.

Hornwort, pondweeds and bladderwort grow in the water and are called submerged aquatics. Water lilies and water plantain are rooting aquatic plants. They grow above the water but have their roots anchored in the mud at the bottom of the pond. These plants have long stems to carry the leaves and flowers above the surface of the water. The stems have air spaces in them to let oxygen pass from the leaves to the roots.

The growth of pond plants is controlled by various substances dissolved in the water. You'll find more about this on page 28. You can find out which substances help growth and which slow down growth by doing some simple tests with duckweed.

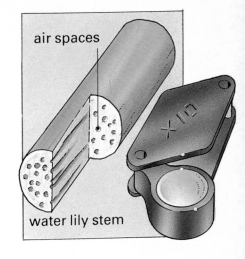

air spaces

water lily stem

△ The cut stem of a water lily.

▽ Half fill four plastic tubs with pond water. Number each tub from 1 to 4. Don't add anything to tub 1. Add a drop of plant food to tub 2, a drop of vinegar to tub 3 and a pinch of sodium bicarbonate to tub 4.

Float ten duckweed leaves in each tub and watch how they grow.

duckweed

pond water

1

2

3

4

13

Making a pond

If you are unable to visit a local pond why not make your own in the garden at home or at school? The most difficult part is digging the hole and you will need some adult help with this. It is important that your pond is large enough not to freeze solid in winter or overheat in summer. It should be about 1 yard square (1 meter square) in area and 20 in (50 cm) deep at its lowest point. Having planned the pond you can now dig the hole.

To make sure the pond is waterproof you can buy a special black plastic sheet large enough to line the hole. Make sure that the edge is level and remove any sharp stones. To prevent the plastic from being punctured spread a layer of fine sand or peat over all the surface of the hole. Place the liner over the hole and hold down the edges with stones.

Fill the pond with water and trim the edge of the liner, leaving 12 in (30 cm) overlap. Cover this with turf or paving stones to keep it in place.

△ An easier but more expensive pond can be made using a molded fiberglass liner. This could be raised above soil level, supported by stones packed with soil. This type of pond will be safer if you have younger brothers and sisters.

Look at the water through polarizing sunglasses which reduce surface glare and make it easier to see what is below.

14

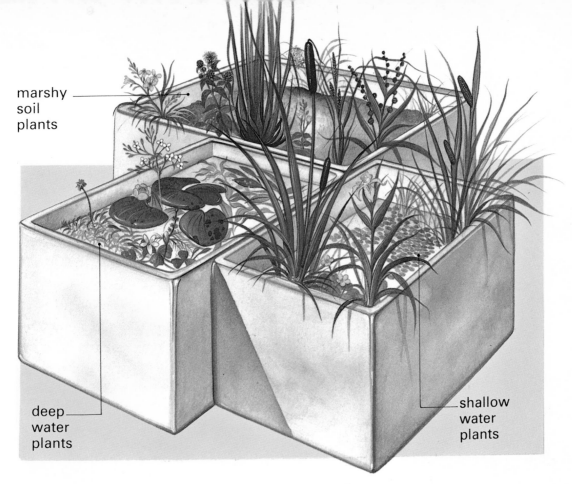

marshy
soil
plants

deep
water
plants

shallow
water
plants

△ If space is limited you could use old sinks to make various wet areas.

One could have just water and free-floating plants. In a second put some soil, shallow water and rooted plants like cattails, blue flag and rushes.

In the third, create a marshy soil with rushes and sedges.

Place the sinks out of direct sunlight and keep them watered regularly.

Stocking the pond

Allow the pond water to stand for 48 hours before putting in any plants or animals. Remember not to take plants from the wild. Try to get some from a friend with a pond or from garden centers which also sell water plants. These must be placed in (or around) the pond at the right depth.

Grow rooted plants in old pots with a layer of stones on the surface to keep the soil in place. Have plenty of submerged plants as these help to oxygenate the water.

Once the plants are established you can introduce animals like pond snails, mussels and water fleas. Only add fish when the pond is one year old. In autumn cover the pond with netting to prevent leaves falling into the water.

15

Amphibians

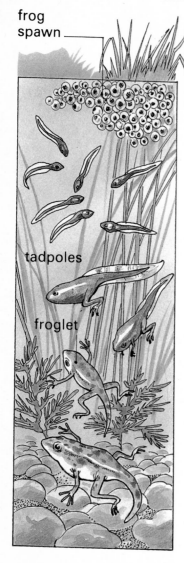

frog spawn

tadpoles

froglet

Frogs will become regular visitors to your pond each spring. Although they live on land they need to return to water to breed. Frogs are amphibians, as are toads and newts, and have permanently wet skin, so always handle them with damp hands.

Frogs mate in the spring and a clump of frog spawn may contain as many as 4,000 eggs. Each egg is coated with a layer of jelly substance which protects the eggs from frost and enables the eggs to float to the surface of the water to be nearer the sun.

adult frog

△ The round black eggs change into comma shapes. Tadpoles emerge from the jelly after ten days and cling to its surface. Soon they feed on algae. Hind legs appear and they feed on small pond animals. Front legs grow and a froglet is formed.

△ Froglets need to breathe air and they come to the surface regularly. The tail shrinks and the froglets come out of the water.

Put a large stone in the bowl for them to crawl on. Once they start jumping return them to the pond.

△ Although they need to keep damp the tiny frogs can now live on land. They can change skin color to match the surroundings, enabling them to hide from predators. Frogs feed on insects which they catch on the sticky tips of their tongues.

Observing and recording

You can record the daily changes in frog spawn by putting some eggs into two bowls of pondwater. Never collect a whole clump of eggs.

Keep one bowl inside a building and the other outside. Note down the dates and what you observe each day in both bowls. You will be able to see how warmth affects the development of tadpoles.

Toads have a warty skin and can live in much drier places—like holes in the ground. Toads mate in water like frogs, but their eggs are in long strings. Newts look like smooth lizards and spend quite some time in the water. They lay their eggs singly under leaves of pond plants.

Frogs and toads have distinctive songs which you could listen to and record, if you have a tape recorder. Make notes in a note book of when the frogs first become active and how many you have spotted.

▽ While the tadpoles are feeding on weeds put some of them in a jam jar of pond water.

Tie small pieces of beef on to lengths of cotton thread. Hang these in the water suspended from a pencil. Watch the tadpoles feed and grow. Compare these with tadpoles feeding only on pondweed.

Don't leave meat in water too long or it will go bad.

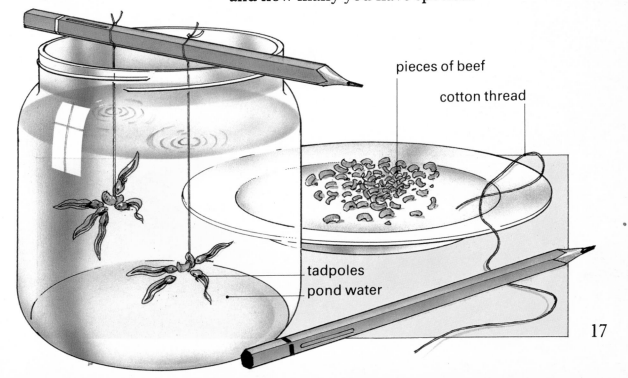

pieces of beef

cotton thread

tadpoles
pond water

Water on the move

A stream is water on the move. As it rushes across the countryside it cuts or erodes a notch or valley for itself. To see the effect of water erosion look for a bend in the stream. The bank on the outside of the bend is being cut away. Debris is deposited on the inside bank creating a beach.

Find out how fast the water is flowing by marking a 5 yd (5 m) length of stream with stakes. Note the time taken for a small piece of wood to float this distance. Divide the time by five to give the rate of flow in seconds per yard (meter).

▽ Take your pond kit to a shallow stream. Use the sieve to disturb the bottom and catch any animals as the water flows through. Lift out stones and check for clinging creatures. Put the stones back in the same place in the stream bed.

Stream life

Animals that live in streams have to be able to survive the current. They are either strong swimmers like freshwater shrimps and fish or clingers like leeches and flatworms.

Flowing water is better at taking oxygen from the air than still water. Animals must have oxygen to breathe and many stream creatures need lots of it.

The plants are firmly rooted in the stream bed or securely attached to stones. They have long stems and like water milfoil finely divided leaves which do not obstruct the water's flow. Some plants like broad-leaved pondweed have fine submerged leaves and broad floating leaves.

Instead of a plan you can draw a stream profile to show the shape of the stream bed. Tie a knotted cord across the stream. Use a level to check that the cord is horizontal.

Start at one end to measure from each knot to the ground using a marked pole. Record each height on a chart. Use the results to plot a graph of the shape of the stream bed and its banks.

△ Fish like sticklebacks and elvers (young eels) weave their way among the weeds.

Mayfly and stonefly nymphs dart around while snails and flatworms glide over the stones.

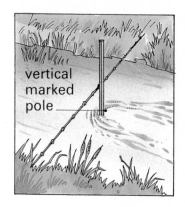

vertical marked pole

△ The cord is knotted at 8 in (20 cm) intervals before it is tied across the stream.

Make sure the stream depth is safe before you start. Try to share this activity with a friend or an adult.

Investigating fish

Everyone who dips in a pond or stream hopes to catch a fish, but they are not always easy to find. Fish are sensitive to movement and vibrations.

They can feel you walking along the bank and see your shadow if it falls on the water. Attract the fish by baiting with small pieces of bread or worms. Some fish always rise to take insects which land accidentally on the surface and become trapped. Insects struggling to escape attract these fish. This is imitated in fly-fishing. Other fish stay near the bottom of the pond, feeding on insects and snails.

Find a bridge over a clear fast-flowing stream. Watch how the fish swim against the current. They are well camouflaged to avoid predators and have more streamlined shapes than fish in ponds.

△ You can see the water ripple as fish rise to take insects.

▽ Catch a fish and put it in a large bowl of water. Watch how it swims then return it to the water.

Setting up an aquarium

To understand how pond creatures live together you can set up a freshwater aquarium. Any large bowl can be used but a glass-sided tank is easier to view.

Cleanliness will prevent disease, so rinse the tank, gravel and stones really well before use. Place a sloping layer of gravel over the bottom of the tank.

Create a landscape using hard stones like granite or sandstone. Plants like broad-leaved pondweed, hornwort and water milfoil can be anchored in the gravel using stones. Wash the plants first and remove any damaged parts.

If you collect plants from a local pond make sure you have the owner's permission, or you can buy some from an aquarium shop.

Add the water as shown and leave the tank to settle for at least a week. You can now put animals in, but remember that diving beetles and dragonfly nymphs are carnivores and will attack the other creatures in your aquarium.

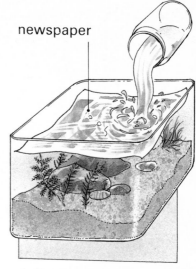

newspaper

△ Having arranged the gravel and plants in the tank, cover them with a layer of newspaper.

Pour water which has stood for a day on to the newspaper. The newly planted tank will not be disturbed by the flow of water.

Place your tank in a well lit place but avoid full sunlight.

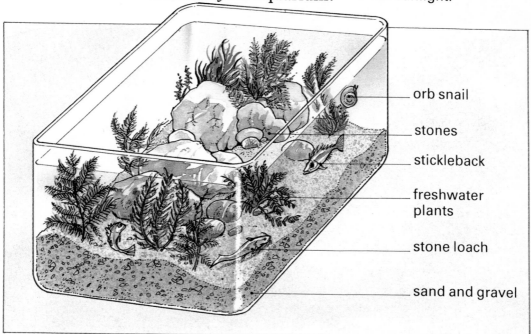

orb snail

stones

stickleback

freshwater plants

stone loach

sand and gravel

Water birds

Early spring is the best time to watch water birds. The males develop special, brightly colored breeding plumage. These are part of a courtship display to attract a mate. Male mallards dive, flap their wings, whistle and grunt. The female responds by jerking her head back and forth.

Once the partnership is established nest building begins. Use binoculars and observe what material is used and how the nest is built. Never disturb nesting birds. If the nest is not hidden you might be able to count the eggs.

Many ducklings swim and feed themselves soon after hatching. Parent birds continue to look after the chicks until they are able to fly.

▽ Keep a weekly diary of all the birds around your stretch of water. You will learn which are visitors. Geese and migrating ducks are seen in winter, swallows and warblers in summer.

cormorant

wood ducks

heron

rail

▽ If you keep a bird diary it is useful to be able to refer quickly to a particular part of the pond.

Divide your pond plan with a grid and letter each square. Use the letters when recording the position of birds.

heron

swallow

Canada geese

How water birds feed

Water is the source of food for many birds. Swallows flying over the surface catch insects as they emerge from the water and dip their beaks into the water to drink.

Ducks can be divided into two groups, the dabblers which up-end and reach down to feed and the divers which disappear underwater. Divers emerge some distance away from where they went down. The shoveler has a wide bill specially adapted to sieve food from the water and mud.

Watch for the heron standing sentinel on its long stilt-like legs. It feeds on fish, frogs and water beetles.

Many birds are hidden in the reeds but can be recognized by their calls. You may hear the deep boom of a bittern sounding like a distant fog-horn or the warning call of a coot which reacts when its territory is invaded.

23

Mammals

Mammals around ponds and streams are very shy. You must be really quiet if you want to observe them. Make sure you are facing into the wind, otherwise your scent will be carried ahead of you and warn the animals that you are approaching.

Look for signs of meadow voles. These are herbivores, so nibbled plant stems show where they feed. A meadow vole often sits and grooms on a raft of floating water plants. A hole in the bank just above the water level could belong to a meadow vole or a water shrew. The water shrew has a grey velvety coat and feeds on insects, small fish and frogs.

▽ Meadow voles and water shrews spend almost as much time in the water as on land. They find most of their food in the water.

Many harvest mice have left the fields and prefer to live in the safer habitat of sedges and rushes beside ponds and streams.

harvest mouse

meadow vole

water shrew

▷ Beavers are common in North America. They fell trees by gnawing through the trunks in order to dam streams. The beaver's home, called a lodge, is found among the trunks and branches of the dam.

beaver

mink

▷ Mink are predators on muskrats, fishes and frogs. Their dark brown coats which look black when wet. They live in holes in stream banks.

Nests and tracks

Among the tall reeds and sedges, look for the nest of the harvest mouse, one of the smallest mammals. About 12 in (30 cm) above the ground, the nest is made of a ball of interwoven leaves. It is much easier to find a nest in the winter when the plants have died.

Find a shallow muddy bank and look for animal tracks in the mud. The paired "slots" of deer are very obvious. Along a stream, try to find the place where other mammals like foxes and raccoons cross.

If you are very lucky you might find the tracks of an otter. This nocturnal mammal feeds on fish and frogs. It leaves its droppings, called scats, on a rock or tussock of grass.

More often seen and mistaken for an otter is the mink. Originally these escaped from fur farms and now breed in the wild in Britain. In some parts of Europe they have been deliberately released along with coypus and muskrats.

△ The otter has a broad muzzle and flat head. With webbed feet, thick tail and waterproof fur it is well adapted to life in water.

25

Food webs

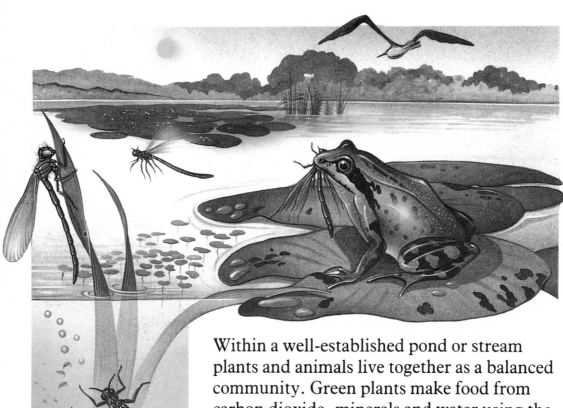

△ This shows a typical food chain. Algae in the water are eaten by water fleas. Damselfly nymphs eat the water fleas. As adults, damselflies are eaten by a frog which is caught by a heron.

Work out food chains for your pond. Try to join them to make a food web.

Within a well-established pond or stream plants and animals live together as a balanced community. Green plants make food from carbon dioxide, minerals and water using the sun's energy. They are called producers.

Plants are eaten by some pond animals (the herbivores) like snails and caddisfly larvae. Backswimmers, leeches and dragonfly nymphs are meat eaters (carnivores). They prey on the herbivores. Fishes, birds and mammals feed on these carnivores.

Animals depend on the food made by green plants and are called consumers. In this way a food chain is formed, linking the producers with all the consumers. A simple food chain would be: pondweed → pond snail → leech → diving beetle. Most consumers feed on a variety of foods, so different food chains are linked to form a food web.

How water is colonized

Most ponds have existed for some time and show well developed animal and plant communities. But food chains begin very early in a pond's life.

You can look at this by keeping a bowl of rain water outside and watching what happens to the water. First to appear are the algae. These tiny plants cause the water to turn green. Single-celled creatures called protozoans appear next and feed on the algae.

Soon animals like rotifers and water fleas appear and eat the protozoans. All these first colonizers have drought resistant spores or eggs which are carried by the wind. Flying insects like mosquitoes and gnats lay their eggs on the water. These hatch into aquatic larvae which feed on the first colonizers.

▽ Take a shallow bowl half-filled with water. Put in a handful of hay and leave the bowl outside. Each day take samples with a dropper. You can try to identify the larger organisms with a hand lens but in the early stages you will need a microscope.

Draw the organisms you see and record the dates when they appear. This record will show how the pond gets its plants and animals.

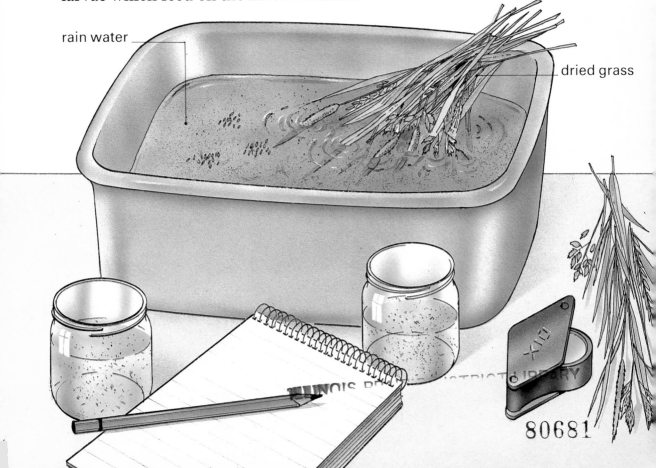

rain water

dried grass

Pollution

Anything which upsets the delicate balance of organisms living in fresh water is a pollutant. This may be a poisonous chemical from a factory draining into a nearby stream.

Excess nutrients dissolved in the water cause a different problem, as the algae grow very rapidly forming a green "bloom" in the water. Once the nutrients are used the algae die. As the dead algae decay, this process takes the oxygen from the water, leaving none for the animals. They suffocate and die.

There are two sources of dissolved oxygen in fresh water. One is from the air, the other is from submerged plants which produce oxygen during photosynthesis. The oxygen supply can be reduced by too many ducks eating and disturbing the pondweed.

▽ Water can be polluted in several different ways:
(1) Overhanging trees reduce light and their leaves fall into the water.
(2) Chemicals from factories drain into streams.
(3) Soluble fertilizers drain off the farmers' fields and into ponds or streams.
(4) Garbage dumped in ponds.

△ Many ponds have been improved by the removal of garbage. You will need adult help if your local pond needs to be cleared.

Acid rain

A recent problem is acid rain. Gases produced by coal and oil-burning factories and power stations contain acid substances. These pass into the atmosphere and are carried by the wind.

In the clouds they dissolve in water droplets which fall to the ground as acid rain. Many northern lakes and those in southern Norway, Sweden and in western Europe have been affected and some have no living creatures in them at all.

In surveys of ponds and streams observers can detect whether the water is polluted by identifying certain creatures. They are called "indicator" species. Stonefly nymphs are only found in clean water, while polluted water contains mosquito larvae, bloodworms and rat-tailed maggots. But if it is very badly polluted, the water contains nothing at all.

You could find out whether or not your local pond or stream is polluted.

Glossary

Life cycle of caddisfly

eggs

1

larva

2

pupa

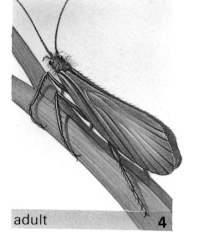

3

△ An example of complete metamorphosis. (1) The adult insect lays eggs on pondweed. (2) The larvae hatch and make cases which are their special homes. (3) When fully grown the larva pupates in the case. (4) In spring the adult emerges.

Algae
The simplest group of plants, ranging from one-celled forms to large seaweeds.

Amphibians
A group of back-boned animals which spend most of their life on land but need water to reproduce; for example frogs, toads and newts.

Bacteria
Very simple organisms of microscopic size that are the main agents of decay.

Camouflage
The ability of an animal to change its color to blend in with or match its surroundings.

Carnivore
An animal which eats other animals.

Colonization
The process by which an organism arrives at and lives in a place not previously inhabited.

Environment
The surroundings in which an organism lives.

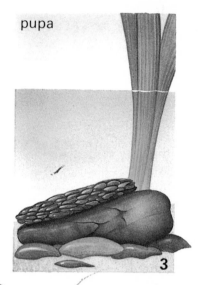

adult

4

Fungi
Simple plants that lack any green coloring. They are one of the main agents of decay.

Habitat
The special kind of environment in which a particular animal or plant lives.

Herbivore
An animal that feeds on plants.

Metamorphosis
The changes in form that occur during the life cycle of certain animals. For example in the frog the egg hatches into a tadpole which gradually changes into an adult. This also happens in insects as is described for the caddisfly and dragonfly.

Nutrients
Substances that enable organisms to grow.

Organism
Any living animal or plant.

Oxygen
A gas in air needed by all living organisms to breathe so that they can release energy from food.

Photosynthesis
The process by which green plants make food (sugar) from carbon dioxide and water. Sunlight is the energy source and oxygen is released during the process.

Predator
Animal which hunts and feeds upon another animal.

Vegetation
All the plants growing in a particular place.

▽ An example of incomplete metamorphosis. (1) The adult insect lays eggs in the water. (2) These hatch into nymphs which are like small wingless forms of the adult. (3) As they grow they shed their skins in a series of molts. From the final molt the adult insect emerges.

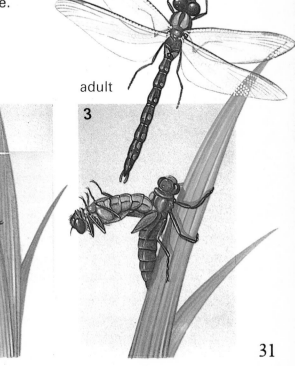

adult

1 eggs

2

nymph

3

Life cyle of dragonfly

31

Index